A BUG'S DAY

A Honeybee's Day

by Elizabeth Neuenfeldt
Illustrated by Claudia Marianno

BLASTOFF! MISSIONS

BLASTOFF! MISSIONS, AN IMPRINT OF BELLWETHER MEDIA BY FLUTTERBEE

Blastoff! Missions takes you on a learning adventure! Colorful illustrations and exciting narratives highlight cool facts about our world and beyond. Read the mission goals and follow the narrative to gain knowledge, build reading skills, and have fun!

Traditional Nonfiction

Narrative Nonfiction

Blastoff! Universe

MISSION GOALS

- FIND YOUR SIGHT WORDS IN THE BOOK.
- LEARN ABOUT THE DIFFERENT ROLES OF HONEYBEES.
- LEARN ABOUT WHAT A HONEYBEE DOES IN A DAY.

This edition first published in 2027 by Bellwether Media, Inc.

For information regarding permission, write to Bellwether Media, Inc., Attention: Permissions Department, 3500 American Blvd W, Suite 150, Bloomington, MN 55431.

Library of Congress Cataloging-in-Publication Data

Names: Neuenfeldt, Elizabeth author | Marianno, Claudia, illustrator. Title: A honeybee's day / by Elizabeth Neuenfeldt; illustrated by Claudia Marianno.
Description: Minneapolis, Minnesota : Bellwether Media, Inc., [2026] | Series: A bug's day | Includes bibliographical references and index. | Audience: Ages 5-8 | Audience: Grades 2-3 | Summary: "Vibrant illustrations accompany information about honeybees. The narrative nonfiction text is intended for students in kindergarten through third grade."-- Provided by publisher.
Identifiers: LCCN 2026001550 (print) | LCCN 2026001551 (ebook) | ISBN 9798898800888 (library binding) | ISBN 9798898802127 (ebook)
Subjects: LCSH: Honeybee--Behavior--Juvenile literature | Honeybee--Juvenile literature | Bees--Juvenile literature | Insects--Juvenile literature
Classification: LCC QL568.A6 N475 2026 (print) | LCC QL568.A6 (ebook)
LC record available at https://lccn.loc.gov/2026001550
LC ebook record available at https://lccn.loc.gov/2026001551 =

Editor: Betsy Rathburn Designer: Laura Sowers

Printed in the United States of America, North Mankato, MN.

This is **Blastoff Jimmy**! He is here to help you on your mission and share fun facts along the way!

Table of Contents

In the Hive

JIMMY SAYS

A honeybee colony can have more than 80,000 honeybees!

The honeybee **colony** is waking up. Time for another busy day in the **hive**!

Those **worker bees** are ready to start their day.

Those young worker bees clean the hive's **cells**. Later, they will help build new cells.

Each cell is like a room.
Cells can store food and eggs!

queen
egg

Here comes the **queen**! She lays eggs in cells.

Those worker bees give her food. **Drones** will **mate** with her.

It is time to leave the hive. Those workers guard the entrance.

Their **stingers** keep danger away. They look out for skunks and bears. Good luck, workers!

Finding Flowers

It is a sunny morning in the forest. The workers' strong wings help them fly between trees.

There is a field nearby.
Will it have food?

JIMMY SAYS

Honeybees fly around 15 miles (24 kilometers) per hour.

Wow! This field is full of flowers!

These flowers have tasty **nectar**. The workers use their straw-like tongues to drink it. The bees store the nectar for later.

The workers gather **pollen** from flowers for the hive. It sticks to the bees' fuzzy legs.

Some pollen falls off
at the next flower.
This helps flowers grow!

Heading Home

The sun is going down.
Time to go home!

The worker bees bring pollen and nectar back to the hive. Most of the pollen will be food for **larvae**.

The worker bees give the nectar to younger workers. They put it in cells. They will make it into honey.

It has been a long day for these busy bees!

All About Honeybees

Body Parts

Things Seen

hive

flowers

honey

Glossary

cells–small areas in honeybee hives that hold food, eggs, and larvae

colony–a group of honeybees

drones–male bees that mate with queen bees

hive–the home of a honeybee colony

larvae–young insects that break out of eggs and look like small worms

mate–to join together to make young

nectar–a sweet liquid that comes from plants

pollen–a fine dust found in plants that is carried to other plants of the same kind to make seeds

queen–a female honeybee that lays eggs for its hive

stingers–sharp body parts that honeybees use to attack enemies

worker bees–female honeybees that gather food, care for the queen, and feed larvae

To Learn More

AT THE LIBRARY

Grack, Rachel. *Bee Hives.* Minneapolis, Minn.: Bellwether Media, 2026.

Kenney, Karen Latchana. *All About Bees.* Minneapolis, Minn.: Jump!, 2024.

Pettiford, Rebecca. *Honeybees.* Minneapolis, Minn.: Bellwether Media, 2025.

ON THE WEB

FACTSURFER

Factsurfer.com gives you a safe, fun way to find more information.

1. Go to www.factsurfer.com.
2. Enter "a honeybee's day" into the search box and click .
3. Select your book cover to see a list of related content.

BEYOND THE MISSION

> WHAT FACT FROM THE BOOK DID YOU THINK WAS THE MOST INTERESTING?

> DRAW A HONEYBEE. WHICH BODY PARTS DO YOU THINK ARE MOST IMPORTANT?

> HONEYBEES DO MANY JOBS. WHICH JOB DO YOU THINK IS MOST IMPORTANT?

Index